Contents

Before You Begin   4

Part 1—Drawing Animals   5
Alligator • Bear • Beaver • Bird • Bison (Buffalo) • Bunny • Cat •
Chicken • Baby Chicks • Clam/Oyster • Crab • Dog • Dolphin •
Duck • Fish • Hippopotamus • Lion • Monkey • Mouse • Owl •
Parrot • Penguin • Pig • Porcupine • Sheep • Skunk • Tiger •
Turtle • Walrus

Part 2—Drawing People   66
Smiling Faces—Female • Angry Faces—Female • Smiling Faces—
Male • Angry Faces—Male • Hairstyles—Male and Female •
Clothes, Costumes, and Uniforms • Partial Views • Body Shapes—
Male • Body Shapes—Female • Body Shapes—Stretched • Body
Shapes—Babies • Hands • Hands Intertwined • Arms • Arms and
Legs • People Sitting • Movement • Motion Lines • Unusual
Positions

Caption Balloons   125

About the Author   127

Index   128

Before You Begin

Everyone likes to draw cartoons, but some people think they have to be trained artists to draw them. That's just not true. Anyone can draw great cartoons.

The important thing to remember is that cartoonists have to THINK FUNNY. In fact, being able to think funny is even more important for a cartoonist than being able to draw well. That's because cartoons have their origin in humor rather than art.

This book is filled with step-by-step instructions for drawing cartoon animals and people. There are also lots of ideas for things you can add to your drawings to make them even MORE fun.

As you draw along, remember that you can always add your own ideas. Keep thinking funny and you'll find that your cartoons will get better and better.

Do you have a pencil and some paper ready? Great! Then let's start drawing…

Cartooning for Kids

Mike Artell

STERLING PUBLISHING CO., INC.
NEW YORK

Library of Congress Cataloging-in-Publication Data Available

10/12

20   19

First paperback edition published in 2002 by
Sterling Publishing Co., Inc.
387 Park Avenue South, New York, NY 10016
© 2001 by Mike Artell
Distributed in Canada by Sterling Publishing
c/o Canadian Manda Group, 165 Dufferin Street,
Toronto, Ontario, Canada M6K 3H6
Distributed in Great Britain and Europe by Chris Lloyd at Orca Book
Services, Stanley House, Fleets Lane, Poole BH15 3AJ, England
Distributed in Australia by Capricorn Link (Australia) Pty. Ltd.
P.O. Box 704, Windsor, NSW 2756, Australia

Sterling ISBN-13: 978-1-4027-0111-5
          ISBN-10: 1-4027-0111-X

For information about custom editions, special sales, premium and
corporate purchases, please contact Sterling Special Sales
Department at 800-805-5489 or specialsales@sterlingpub.com.

PART 1

Drawing Animals

Alligator

We'll start by drawing an alligator. Alligators have strong muscles that snap their jaws shut. But the muscles that open their mouths are very weak. It's easy to hold their mouths shut. Just don't let go!

Begin your gator by drawing the nostrils and a bumpy snout.

Add the top of the mouth.

Now we need some big, round eyes.

Draw a curved line from below the front of the snout to the back of the right eye.

Now add the back. Just draw some up-and-down points.

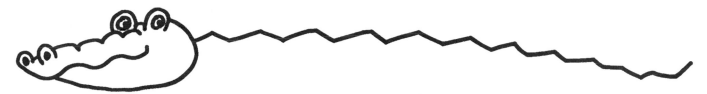

The next step is to add short, fat legs and a chest.

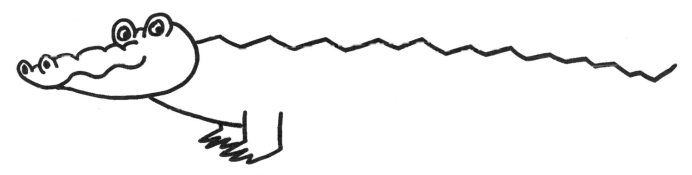

Draw a stomach and some more short, fat legs.

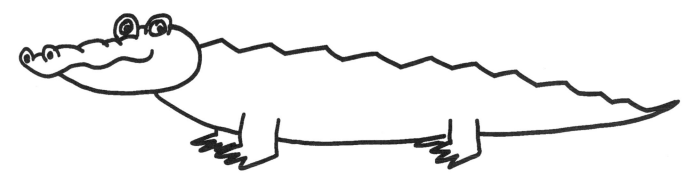

Connect a line from the back leg to the top of the tail.

For a finishing touch, you can add some scales and some lines on the gator's stomach.

You can also hide your alligator in the water...

Or you can draw your alligator chasing some dinner.

UH-OH!

LOOK OUT!

Bear

Scientists have identified eight different kinds of bears: polar bears, brown bears, American black bears, giant panda bears, Asian black bears, sloth bears, sun bears, and spectacled bears.

Let's draw a baby brown bear cub. Begin by drawing the face. The nose is shaped like a triangle and the eyes are close together. Add a little curved line for a mouth.

The head is wide at the top and narrow in the face. Add two ears that are almost square-shaped.

Now we need two bumps for the back. The first bump is small, the second bump is larger.

Now add a back leg and a foot.

The front leg is thick. You'll also need to draw a little line between the legs for a stomach.

The chest and front left leg are a series of bumps followed by a straight line, then a pointy foot. It sounds harder than it really is. Just draw two bumps under the bear cub's face, a line for the leg, then the foot.

Color the nose, add some background, and you've drawn a bear cub.

But be careful, the bear cub's mom might be close by.

Beaver

Beavers have two large front teeth that never stop growing. That's why they have to keep grinding them down by chewing on trees and other plants.

We'll draw a triangular nose, dot eyes, and round cheeks. Add two big teeth.

Give your beaver some hair on its head and two round ears. Draw an open mouth behind the teeth.

Draw some "grassy" lines to give the beaver a rounded back. Add one arm and hand.

This beaver is going to be holding a little snack. It's a small branch from a tree. Draw the branch and add three fingers at the bottom. Don't forget to draw a little of the beaver's other arm. Now draw a fuzzy chest and tummy.

This beaver has big back legs and long toes. Add them now.

And of course, everyone knows that a beaver has a big flat tail.

13

Bird

There are many different kinds of birds. Some are big, like the ostrich that can grow as tall as nine feet (3m). Others are small like hummingbirds that are only a few inches long. We're going to draw a mama bird and a baby bird in a nest.

 Begin by drawing a pointy head and a skinny neck.

 Add a straight back and a triangle-shaped tail.

 Now, draw a rounded chest and back side.

 Add a little wing.

Let's add a baby bird.
Draw a round head
and add a beak that
looks like the letter "M"
tilted to the side.

Add a "dot" eye
and a skinny neck.

A quick way to draw the
nest is to make lots of
criss-cross lines—sort
of like the letter "X."

Add a few eggs to complete your drawing. What do you think the
baby bird is saying to its mama?

Bison (Buffalo)

Even though bison look heavy and slow, they can run faster than 30 miles per hour. Here's a bison that you can draw.

Start with the nose and mouth.

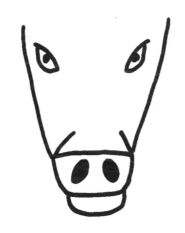

The head slants in from the top. The eyes are shaped a little like tree leaves. Add a dot in each eye.

Give your bison a beard and some horns.

Next, add lots and lots of curly hair on your bison's head. Draw two ears, too.

The bison has a large bump on its back. Draw the bump with a "grassy" line.

Do the same for your bison's chest. Use a "grassy" linc. This is one way to draw fur.

The back end of this cartoon bison is much smaller than the front end.

Add two legs and a tail. Draw some more "grassy" lines where the bison's stomach is.

Now add the legs on the other side of the bison's body.

Mountains and grass make a nice background.

Bunny

They're cute. They're fluffy. They're bunnies! Even though bunnies have big front teeth, they're not rodents. They are members of a family of animals called *Lagomorphs.* **Most pet bunnies live from 5 to 8 years.**

To draw a bunny, start by drawing the head, nose, and eyes. Notice that the head has a large bump at the top and a smaller bump near the nose. The mouth comes out of the bottom bump.

The ears are long and rounded on the ends.

Next, add a rounded back. Make this round line start from the side of the ear. Add one foot on the side closest to you. Draw part of the foot on the other side.

What's left? A back leg, a tummy, and a fluffy tail. Draw some lines inside the ears too.

If you draw the ears going down, you get a floppy-eared bunny.

Bunnies are usually very shy. Here's one peeking out from its hutch.

Cat

Cats have eyes that are especially good for seeing when there's not much light. But did you know that cats can't see things that are right under their noses? That's why they sometimes don't see the little treats you put on the floor in front of them.

You can draw a cat if you follow these steps:

Draw a triangle nose, a little "beard," and two puffy cheeks. Now add some round eyes and draw straight lines inside the eyes.

Cats have great hearing. Give your cat some big ears and a fuzzy head. Add whiskers, too.

The next thing your cat needs is a round back and two front legs. Add some fur under the head to make the chest fuzzy.

The last step is to add a back leg and a long tail. Don't forget to draw a little bit of the back leg on the other side, too. Add some zigzag lines for fur on the kitty's tummy.

Chicken

This chicken is basically shaped like a big, puffy cloud. Believe it or not, there are more chickens in the world than there are people. Isn't that egg-citing?

Start with a triangle beak and two dot eyes.

Add bumps on the top of the chicken's head. Also draw some bumps on one side of the head.

Add bumps on the other side of the head.

Now draw some wings. They look like the bumps you draw when you draw a cloud.

Now bring the bumps around the bottom of the chicken. Keep it rounded.

Add some eggs underneath and a few pieces of hay.

Baby Chicks

Now let's draw some simple little cartoon chicks to go along with your chicken. Ever wonder what a baby chick does for food while it's growing in the egg? Surprise! The baby chick gets its nourishment from the egg yolk. That's the yellow part of the egg.

The face of the chick looks exactly like the face of the chicken—triangle beak and two dot eyes.

Next, draw a big, fuzzy circle around the face of the chicken. The fuzz looks a lot like grass. Add stick legs and three lines for toes.

Complete the cartoon by drawing lots of fuzzy little chicks around their mama.

Clam/Oyster

Scientists once discovered a clam that weighed more than 700 pounds! Whew! That would make a lot of clam chowder.

Here's how to draw a clam. (Psst…it's also how to draw an oyster. They look a lot alike.)

Start with a shape that looks a little like the wing of an airplane.

Add a round, "happy face" shape to the bottom of the first shape.

Draw a little circle on the left side of the clam/oyster. Add eyes.

Color in the area around the eyes. Add some lines to the top of the shell. Add some bubbles too.

Presto! You've drawn a clam…or an oyster…whatever!

Crab

Female blue crabs can produce millions of eggs at a time. Whew! That's a lot of kids! Are you feeling crabby today? If so, maybe drawing a crab will make you feel better.

Start with a wavy line on top.

Add another wavy line on the bottom. So far it looks a little like the top of a pie, doesn't it?

Next, add a "happy face" line to the bottom of the first two lines.

We're going to draw this crab's eyes on the end of "stalks." Just draw two lines coming out of the top of the shell, then add two eyes.

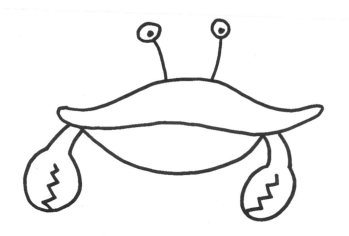

Notice that if you turn up the ends of the shell, it makes your crab look like it's smiling.

Watch out for the claws!!

Connect some little rectangles together to make the crab's legs.

Draw some sand, add a little water, and there's your crab! Good job!

Dog

We all know that dogs have a better sense of smell than humans do—but how much better? BZZZZZ! Sorry, you're out of time! The answer is 1,000 times better!

We'll start drawing our cartoon dog by making a triangle nose. Now add some rounded lines for the area near the mouth.

Draw a tongue and two big, round eyes.

This is one way to draw the ears. You can experiment with the ears by making them longer or shorter.

Your dog needs a long, straight back and a tail. You can also give your dog a little round backside.

Add two legs and feet. Notice how each paw has some lines on it to show the toes.

The last step is to add two more legs and two feet on the other side. Since these legs and feet are partially hidden by the legs closest to us, you only have to draw part of the other two legs and feet.

Is this little guy cute or what?

Look! He's happy to see you! He's wagging his tail.

Guess who just had a bath? This is what happens when you dry your dog with a blow dryer.

Hmmm...Looks like somebody is hungry.

Dolphin

You've probably seen lots of dolphins on television. You may have even seen real dolphins swimming in the ocean. Here's a quick way to draw a dolphin.

Begin by drawing a little "hill." Add a fin on top.

Make a narrow nose. Draw a mouth, and then draw the dolphin's eye low on the head and near the end of its mouth.

Draw a fin on the side. Add a line for the underside of the dolphin. Notice how narrow the back end of the dolphin is. It's very skinny just before the spot where the tail starts.

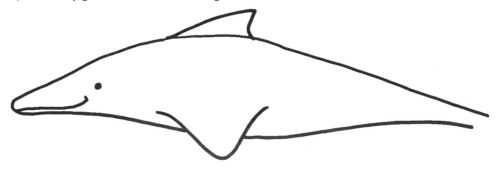

The final step in drawing our dolphin is to add a flat tail and a blow hole on the top of its head.

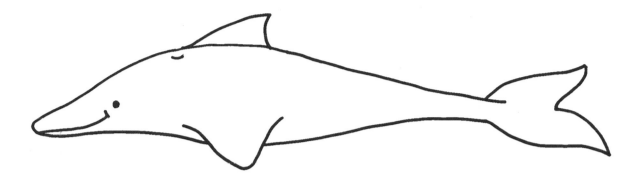

A small group of dolphins is called a "pod." Larger groups are called "schools" or "herds." If you "overlap" several dolphin drawings, you can draw your own dolphin pod.

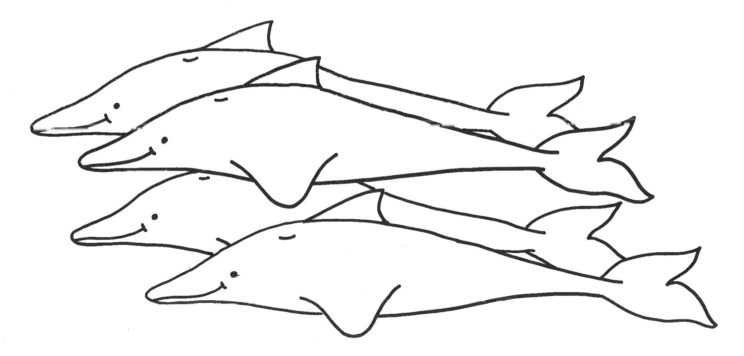

Duck

Just our luck—it's a duck! Female ducks are called hens, just like chickens. But do you know the proper name for a male duck? It's not a rooster—it's a drake!

This duck's head is round. The beak is slanted on the top and flat on the bottom. Add a dot eye.

The back of our cartoon duck is very straight. The tail curves up in the back and the rear end is rounded.

Add a round chest in the front and some water. You're almost done...

Give your duck a band around its neck and a wing. Now add some water. Very good!

If you draw the same duck a little smaller and place it behind the first duck, it will look like a mama duck with one of her ducklings.

Just for fun, draw a mama duck with a long line of ducklings following her.

Fish

There are more than 20,000 different kinds of fish. Here's one that most people have never seen — the rare car-tuna!

Start by drawing a "frowny-face" line for the top of the body. Add a curved line to one end.

Open the mouth and then draw a "happy-face" line for the bottom of the fish.

Now your fish needs a tail and one eye. The other eye is on the other side of the head — we won't see it.

Stick on a few fins and color the inside of the mouth, and you've drawn a fish! Easy, huh?

You can show that your fish is under the water by adding a few bubbles.

Here's a whole school of fish!

Uh-oh…somebody is about to be somebody else's dinner! Notice that both of these fish are drawn the same way. One is just larger than the other.

Hippopotamus

The word "hippopotamus" means "river horse." That's a good name for hippos since they spend so much time in the water.

Begin by drawing this shape.

Notice how narrow the top of the mouth and nose are near the eyes. The top of the head is very round.

Add ears, a bottom jaw, and two big teeth.

The hippo's body is bean-shaped. Add a little tail.

Next, draw some short, thick legs. Give your hippo some toenails, too.

Lion

Lions are big cats. They have excellent hearing and eyesight, but what they're really famous for is their roar. A male lion's roar can be heard as far as 5 miles away. We're going to draw a funny little lion roaring as hard as he can. Ready? Let's draw.

Start with a balloon-shaped head. Add a little beard at the bottom. This lion's eyes will be closed, and its mouth will be open.

Now draw a big fuzzy mane all around the lion's head.

This lion is going to be working hard at his roaring, so we want to draw his arms out to the side, and his hands making fists.

Mr. Lion is standing on his back feet like a human. This makes him seem a little funnier.

Draw a round little body and some short legs. Now add big feet. Draw 3 lines (not lions!) for toes.

The final step is to add a tail and make our lion roar. He thinks he's pretty scary, but to us, he's just a crazy little cartoon.

Monkey

Monkeys belong to a group of animals called primates. Primates include monkeys, apes, and another really weird group of creatures called humans. That's right! People are primates, too.

To draw a monkey, start with a face that looks a little like a 3-leaf clover. Add eyes, nostrils, and a mouth. Notice that the mouth turns up a little in the middle.

Add a lot of fur around the face.

Before you draw this next step, notice the shape of the line. There's a long curvy line for the monkey's back. At the bottom of the back, the line curves back the other way to form the monkey's tail. Take another good look. Okay? Ready to draw?

Draw the monkey's back and tail.

Now it's time to draw the monkey's leg. It looks a little like a human leg. The foot is long and it has long toes. Also add a short line above the leg for the monkey's arm.

Draw the rest of the arm holding a banana. Show a little bit of the other foot and a little of the other hand, too.

Presto! You've drawn a monkey!

43

Mouse

Mice are curious little creatures. They usually come out at night and explore the area near their nests. Even though people think of mice as eating a lot of cheese, their favorite foods are cereal grains and seeds. Here's how to draw a mouse:

Draw the nose, eyes, and ears.

Add a round back.

Now your mouse needs short legs and pointy toes...

And a long, long tail.

EEEK! A mouse!

If you draw a mouse hole with part of the mouse peeking out, you get a cute cartoon.

Here's the same idea using a piece of cheese. The mouse is thinking, "Yum!"

Owl

Whooooo do you think we're going to draw next? Right! It's an owl. Most owls hunt at night, so we don't often get a chance to see them. Watch how easy it is to draw a funny cartoon owl.

Start by drawing a triangle beak and two big, round eyes.

Add a flat head and pointy ears.

Draw two curvy lines for the sides of the owl's body.

Add some little triangle toes. Give your owl some simple wings, too.

Our owl needs a branch to sit on. Add
a pointy branch beneath the owl.

Now draw a tree
trunk and some
leaves, and our
owl is ready to
hunt for some mice.

Parrot

Small parrots live about 10 or 15 years. But some macaws and cockatoos live as long as 75 years! It's not uncommon for them to outlive their owners!

First draw the beak.

Add eyes and a small hole for the nose.

Draw some "spikey" feathers on the parrot's head, then draw a l-o-n-g straight line on a slant for the parrot's back.

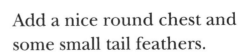

Add a nice round chest and some small tail feathers.

Draw a rounded shape on the parrot's chest and stomach. Draw three lines for the legs.

Add some toes and a perch for your parrot and you're all done!

If you want to color your parrot, use such colors as red, blue, and yellow. Parrots usually have a lot of green in their feathers as well.

Penguin

If you visited the North Pole, how many penguins do you think you'd find? The answer is NONE! That's because all penguins live south of the equator. The penguin we're about to draw will have its wings spread out. Let's go!

Start with a beak that looks like two triangles together. Add a big round eye and a round head. Draw the top of the head close to the eye. Add a neck.

Under the beak, draw a little chin and then add a big, round body. Coming down from the neck on the other side, add a pointy wing.

Now add a wing on the other side of the penguin's body. Draw a curvy line from the penguin's chin, and connect it up with the line that forms the wing. This is a little tricky, so pay close attention to the picture.

We're getting close! All your penguin needs is some webbed feet and a little tail.

If you want to color your penguin, make the head and the edges of its wings black. You can also add a little ice ledge for your penguin to stand on.

Pig

A male pig is called a boar. Do you know the proper name for a female pig? It's a sow.

Start with a flat nose and two dot eyes.

Now, open the mouth and add a round head.

Big, floppy ears would be funny, too. Draw the bottom of the head next.

You can draw the pig's
body lots of ways.
Here's a simple
body. It's just a
big round circle
or egg-shape.

Stick a curly tail on the back side
of your pig and add four skinny legs.

Color in the nostrils
and the mouth.
Add a tongue, too.

There you go!
A perfectly pencilled
porcine.

Porcupine

A large porcupine can have as many as 30,000 quills. We're going to draw a porcupine, but not every quill (thank goodness!).

Start with a simple face like this.

Now start drawing the quills. You can make some of them short near the head, and then make them longer as they move down the back.

The last step is to add some W-shaped feet and a tail. Easy, wasn't it?

54

Sheep

Sheep are gentle creatures that like to stay together in groups. People who take care of sheep are called shepherds. Baby sheep are called lambs. This little sheep may be the simplest animal of all to draw.

Start with a U-shaped head, a Y-shaped nose, and two dot eyes.

Add some fur on the sheep's forehead, and give your sheep two ears.

Now, draw a big, puffy cloud shape all around your sheep.

Draw two front legs and color in the bottom. Now, draw two more legs in the back. Make them a little shorter than the front legs.

If you want to draw the backside of the sheep, just draw the fluffy body and the legs. Then, instead of drawing a head, draw a puffy tail. That's what this cartoon sheep looks like from the rear.

Now...I wonder where Little Bo Peep is?

Skunk

Sniff…sniff…excuse me…do you smell something funny? It might be our next cartoon character.

Start by drawing a head that comes to a point. Add a black nose, two round ears, and two dot eyes.

The legs are short and have pointy toes.

The tail is the most important part of this drawing. Start by making a straight back, then make your line go up into a big arch. Draw another line below it that follows the same shape until it comes to a point at the end of the tail.

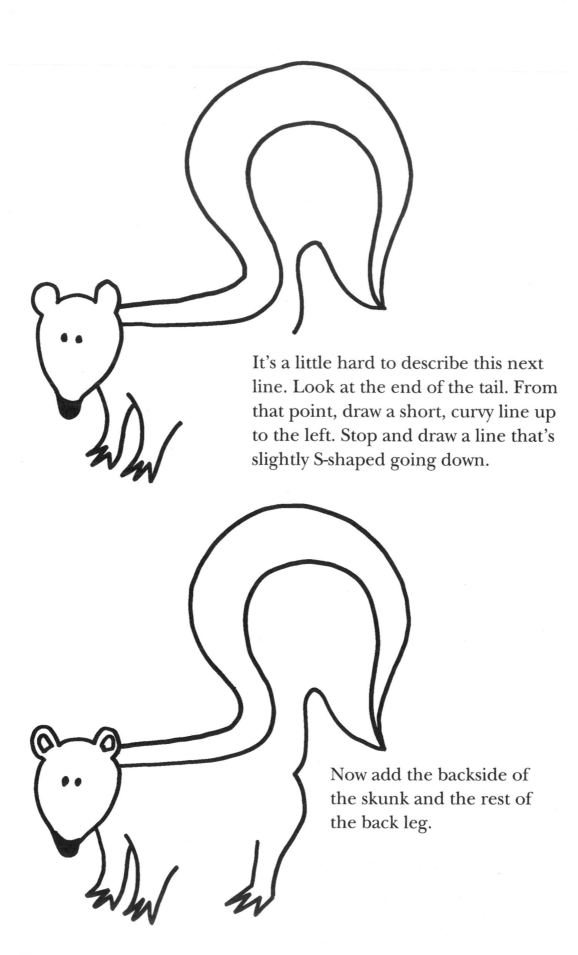

It's a little hard to describe this next line. Look at the end of the tail. From that point, draw a short, curvy line up to the left. Stop and draw a line that's slightly S-shaped going down.

Now add the backside of the skunk and the rest of the back leg.

Connect the front leg to the back leg. Draw part of the other back leg.

Now comes the dramatic part—adding the color. Color everything black except the back, the top of the tail, the face, and the feet.

Add some wavy "stinky" lines and...PEE-YEW! There's your skunk!

Now, let's get out of here!

Tiger

Tigers are members of the cat family. They are also carnivores. That means that the only thing they eat is meat. In fact, the tiger is the largest land animal that eats nothing but meat. Fortunately for us, this cartoon tiger is going to be nice and friendly.

Start with this face…

Draw some pointy ears and some "spikey" hair on the sides of the tiger's head. Add eyebrows, too.

Now, a l-o-o-o-n-g curvy back and a l-o-o-o-n-g tail.

The legs are thick and not too long.

Add some stripes and you have a big, friendly jungle cat.

Turtle

There are more than 250 species of turtle, but you've probably never seen one like the one you're about to draw.

Begin by drawing a head and neck.

Next, add eyes and a shell.

Your turtle needs four legs and a tail. Add them now.

Draw some shapes on your turtle's shell. Add toenails, too.

Z-Z-Z-Z

Here's how to draw a turtle sleeping.

SNAP!

Do you know what kind of turtle this is?

Right! It's a snapping turtle!

Walrus

Walruses like to live where the air and water are cold. They have a thick layer of blubber under their skin that keeps them warm.

To draw a cartoon walrus, start with a triangle nose, two dot eyes, and rounded cheeks.

Add tusks, whiskers, and a round head.

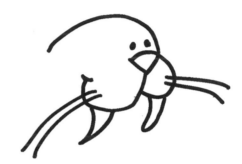

Now, lets draw a big, blubbery body. Make a bump just behind the head, then add a smooth curve for the back.

Draw a round backside for your walrus, too.

Your walrus needs some fins.
Draw a pointy fin for the
front of the walrus
and a flat fin
for the back.

Since this walrus is turned sideways, we'll see only two of its fins.

Add a curved line for the stomach of your walrus, then draw some
background.

Walruses usually like to lie on ice, but sometimes they crawl up on
rocky beaches.

PART 2

Drawing People

Now that you know how to draw animals, it's time to learn how to draw people.

As you draw, keep in mind that we're not trying to create perfect drawings. Our goal is to have some fun and to draw cartoon people that make us laugh. Remember, this is cartooning, not fine art.

Do you have lots of paper and a sharp pencil? Great! Let's draw!

Smiling Faces—Female

On the next few pages, you'll learn how to draw girls and women smiling and laughing. The important thing to remember when you draw female faces is that the noses and chins are generally smaller on female than on males. Often cartoonists draw longer eyelashes on females than on males.

When drawing faces, you always have the option of leaving the eyes open or closed. Sometimes when people smile big (or laugh), their eyes get all squished up. In this section of the book, you'll learn how to draw those squished-up eyes.

If you decide to open the eyes, you'll learn how to draw the rest of the face so it looks even happier.

Here's how it's done…

Begin by drawing this shape.

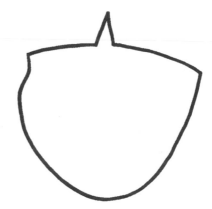

Notice that we didn't begin by drawing a round or oval-shaped head. Instead, we began by drawing the bottom of the head and adding the hair line at the top.

The point at the top of the hair line is the spot where the hair is parted.

Now that we've got the basic shape of the face drawn, you can add the eyes, mouth, and nose. Notice that on this face, the eyes are shut tight. That's because this girl is smiling (or maybe even laughing) and when she smiles, the muscles on her face push up under her eyes and squish her eyes closed.

The neck is the next thing we'll draw. Notice that the neck is curved a little at the bottom. It looks a lot like a tree trunk.

Her shoulders are just two curved lines.

In this example, the collar of the shirt she's wearing is just a straight line. If you prefer, you can make the collar a curved line or any other shape you like.

Now we add the hair on the top and sides of her head. This is a chance for you to really experiment. Draw the hair longer or shorter—whatever style you prefer. Also, try drawing the hair going farther out to the sides. Remember, this is YOUR drawing…you can make it look any way you like.

Now, we're going to draw another smiling female, but we'll give this one a different look.

Let's start by drawing the bottom of the head and add some pointy hair on her brow. This hair looks almost like the sides of a Christmas tree.

Now add the eyes, nose, and mouth.

Notice that the mouth of this character is open a little more than the mouth on your last drawing.

If you draw each eye like a sideways "S," you can give your character some simple eyelashes.

Wow! Look at that hair now! Instead of going straight down on the sides, this hair starts close to the head at the top, then it gets wider and wider as it moves down. Notice that the hair goes straight across at chin level.

Add a neck and collar the way you did in your previous drawing.

Add a little strip of black inside the mouth of this character. When you do this, it shows us the upper and lower teeth.

Just for fun, you can add some accessories. Notice the earrings and glasses? You can experiment with your own earring designs or draw different kinds of glasses. Remember, the goal here is to have some fun, so don't be afraid to experiment with different ideas.

This next smiling female character is going to look VERY different from the other two you just drew.

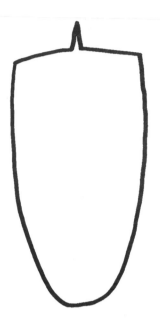

We're going to give this character a very long, narrow face. You can add the hair shown here or you can draw pointy hair on the forehead. Your choice.

Now open the eyes and put two dots in the middle. Add a few short eyelash lines, too. And raise the eyebrows.

When you draw the mouth, open it up really wide. Make it go all the way down to the bottom of the face. Keep the nose small.

Draw lines for the upper and lower teeth. Don't make these lines too big. Try to keep them close to the top and bottom of the mouth. Why? Because the smaller the "teeth" lines are, the more we see of the inside of the mouth. And here we want this character's mouth to be WIDE open.

Draw some oval-shaped ears and add some earrings. You can draw the earrings shown here or create earrings of your own design.

Draw a skinny neck and a collar. By drawing a short little hairstyle, you can exaggerate the shape of this character's face. Color the hair. Add some color to the earrings.

By opening the eyes and the mouth, we have made this character look happy and surprised.

Here are some other happy female faces. Notice the different shapes of the heads, hairstyles, and eyes.

Try experimenting with these elements and see what new kinds of faces you can come up with.

Angry Faces—Female

Those smiling, happy faces were fun, but it's also fun to draw angry faces. In this next section, you'll learn how to change the eyes and mouth to make your characters look angry and upset.

When you draw happy faces, the eyes, eyebrows, and mouths usually go UP. When you draw angry faces, those elements usually go DOWN.

We'll also play with some new head shapes and hairstyles in this section. Ready? Let's go...

This angry girl's head is almost rectangular. It's just rounded a little on the bottom corners.

We'll stick to the hair on the forehead as we've draw it before.

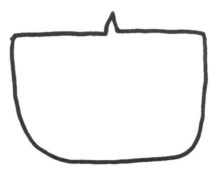

Next, we'll add some angry eyes. Notice how the eyebrows are drawn almost like a wave. The eyes themselves are not complete circles. In fact, the eyes and the nose of this character look the same—except for the fact that the eyes have dots in them. As usual, the nose is small.

The neck is skinnier than usual. The reason we make this neck skinny is to draw attention to the emotion showing on the face. By making the neck skinny, the head looks inflated, and the emotions look more intense.

Now add a rounded collar.

YIKES! Look at that mouth! To make it, you need to draw a shape that is a little like a hot dog that turns down on the ends. Then draw a line across the middle of the mouth and some up-and-down lines, and you'll have little window-shaped teeth.

Notice the addition to the collar and the shoulders. When you draw the shoulders, don't let them come out any farther than the sides of the head.

Give your character a BIG head of dark hair. It adds to the angry look we're trying to draw. The hair looks almost like the opening of a cave: round on top, straight across on the bottom.

We're going to draw some pointy hair on the forehead of this angry character. We're also going to change the shape of the face.

Notice that the face is not completely U-shaped. At the point where the face touches the hair, it's a little narrower. It gets wider near the cheekbones and then it's round on the bottom.

This is another way to draw angry eyes. They look a little like the letter "D" on its side. They're flat on the top and round on the bottom. You can experiment with the size of the eyes to see which you like better—big angry eyes or little ones.

The nose on this character is shaped like one on a happy face. It's a little bigger than the noses we've been drawing.

Experiment with nose sizes to see which you like best.

Now we can add some eyebrows and a mouth. The eyebrows point down, but they don't touch the eyes.

The mouth is shaped like a triangle that's big on one end and small on the other. Round the corners of the triangle a little to make it look more like a real mouth. As you did before, draw a line across the middle of the mouth then draw some up-and-down lines, and you'll have a mouth full of angry teeth.

The hair can be long, short, dark, light, or whatever else you want to draw. This hairstyle is a little more rounded on the bottom than some of the others we've drawn.

The neck is also a little thicker. Try out different hair, necks, and noses to see which ones you like best.

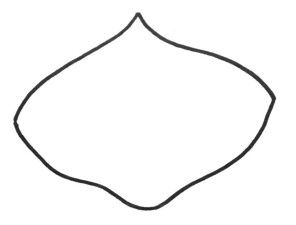

This is a funny shape for a face. It's sort of diamond-shaped. At the bottom of the face is a little round bump. That's the chin.

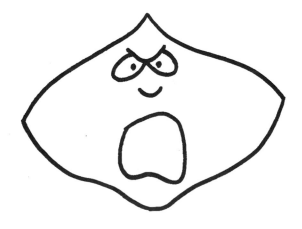

The angry eyes of this character have been squeezed into a small area just under the hair line. The eyebrows are drawn as a single "happy face" line above the eyes.

The mouth is a little larger on one side than the other. It's sort of square-shaped.

It might be fun to draw the teeth a little differently on this character. Last time we made a line straight across the inside of the mouth and then added vertical lines. This time, we are going to draw a curved line across the inside of the mouth.

Now, draw vertical lines that don't match up on either side of the curved line. The vertical lines can be on a slant, too.

Notice the *big* earrings and the pointy collar.

The hair is jelly-bean shaped—big and puffy.

The shoulders don't droop quite as much as some of the previous characters' shoulders. These shoulders go out to the side a little more.

This page shows some other emotions on female characters. Some views are from the front, some are from the side.

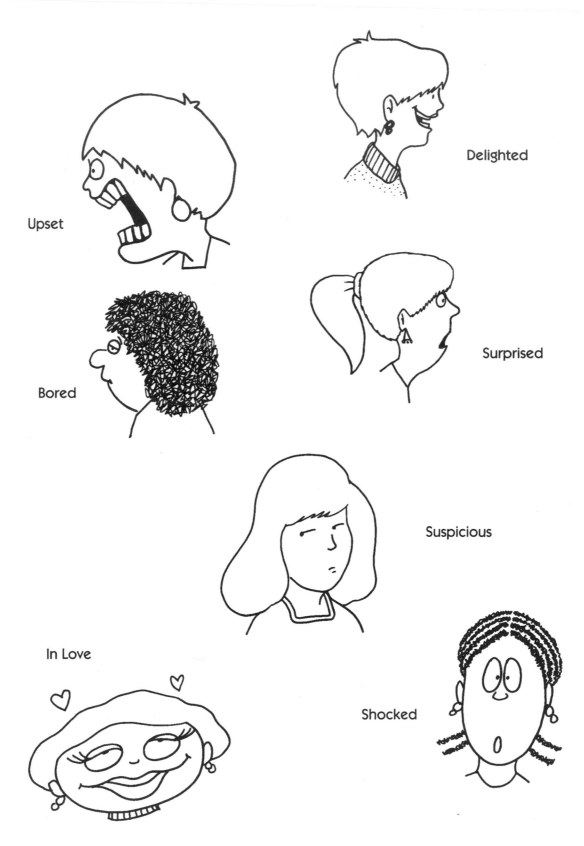

Delighted

Upset

Bored

Surprised

Suspicious

In Love

Shocked

Smiling Faces—Male

Since we all have eyes, noses, and mouths, the emotions
that you draw on female faces can also be drawn on male faces.
Naturally, there are some things people normally associate with
males…for instance, male characters usually (but not always) have
shorter hair than female characters. Also, cartoonists do not
usually draw eyelashes on male characters.

In this section, we'll draw some smiling male faces and have some
fun with the hair, too. On your mark, get set, DRAW!

This little guy's head is going to be VERY wide and not too tall. We'll also draw some nice big ears for him.

Just for fun, draw the neck skinny and short. Add a collar and some little tiny shoulders.

Give him some *big* eyes and add some eyebrows. Draw a little nose.

Now, add a mouth that starts at the top of the eyes and goes all the way across the face and up the other side to the top of the eyes.

Add some small lines at the end of the mouth to show where the cheeks are.

Add the bottom half of the mouth. Start at the cheek and go all the way around to the other side.

Give this character some teeth, too.

We'll finish our drawing by adding some goofy hair. Start just above the ear and "pull" a strand of hair all the way over the top of the head to the other side. Now "pull" some more strands until you have a complete head of hair.

Draw a few pieces of hair bending down to the ear on one side. Draw a few pieces of hair sticking up just above the ear.

That's one crazy-looking character!

This head is completely different from the last one. This character is going to have a huge mouth, so make his face long and squared-off at the bottom.

He's laughing, so squish the eyes closed. Add ears, too.

He'll have some short hair sticking straight up. Just draw some short little lines—sort of like drawing blades of grass.

The mouth is a large rectangle. Make it go all the way down to the bottom of the face.

Instead of making the teeth go all the way across the mouth, we're going to draw them going only part of the way. Draw some rectangular teeth on the left side of the mouth at the top and bottom.

Here's something else that's a little weird! Draw the neck coming out of the side of the head instead of from the bottom of the head. It makes him look as if he's laughing really hard.

Add a round neck on his shirt and some pointy collars.

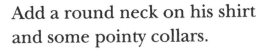

Now, color in his mouth and add some shoulders and part of the body to your character.

HA! It makes you laugh just to look at this guy!

Now it's time to get *really* goofy. Almost everything about this next cartoon character is going to be weird.

Draw this shape.

Notice how big the nose is. The ears are little bumps on the sides of the head.

Once again, we're doing something funny with the mouth and teeth. This guy's smile is so big, it goes almost to the side of his face.

His teeth are only in the middle of the mouth, not all the way across.

His neck is skinny.

Add some curly hair to this character by making a little "nervous" line on his forehead and around from one ear to the other.

Draw another line around his collar and add some small shoulders. Notice that the shoulders do not go out farther than the edge of the face.

Color in the hair. Add a line between the two front teeth to make it look like there's a gap between them.

Draw a line between the chin and the bottom of the mouth to give the impression of a lower lip.

Color in the inside of the mouth.

Every face is different. Here are some examples of smiling male faces that you can draw. After you've drawn these faces, try to come up with your own smiling faces.

Try drawing a few from the side and a few from the front. If you need some ideas for faces, look at people in your family, photos in magazines, or people on TV.

90

Angry Faces—Male

In this section, you'll learn how to draw cartoon characters that are not happy. Some of them will be frowning, others will be growling.

You can use much of what you learned in the earlier sections on angry faces. But this section will also give you some new ideas for different things to do with angry mouths.

Is everybody angry? GOOD! Lct's draw!

This cartoon character has a head that's shaped almost like a diamond—except it's open at the top.

The nose on this character is very large and it's near the top of the head.

Don't forget, you can always experiment with the shapes of heads, noses, eyes, mouths, etc.

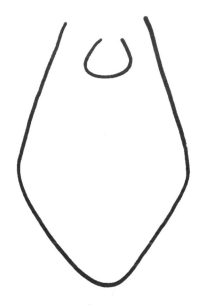

The next step in drawing this angry character is to add some angry eyes. The eyes are actually small, but since they're near the top of the head where it gets smaller, they look large. Make sure you draw really wavy eyebrows.

Add some large ears near the top of the head about the same height as the eyes.

Next, we'll add some scruffy hair. On this character, we've only drawn a little hair. You can draw more hair or you can make him almost bald. It's up to you.

The mouth is *very* large and at a funny angle. By drawing the mouth at this angle, the character will look as if his upper lip is curled up.

When people get angry, they often raise their shoulders up toward their ears. When this happens, it's hard to see their necks. Look at this character…do you see his neck? Nope.

If you draw a line across the middle of this character's mouth, and add big teeth, he'll look *really* angry. If you color in his gums, he'll look angry and *scary*.

This next angry man will have a very different face from the first one, but they will both have their shoulders up near their ears.

Begin by drawing this shape.

Notice the little bump on the bottom of the face. That's his chin.

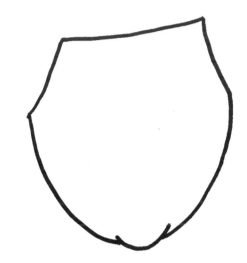

The hair on his forehead is a nice smooth line that has just a little curve in it.

Now you can add some puffy, wavy hair and some ears. Draw some little curvy lines inside of the ears.

Draw the eyebrows on this character as a smooth "happy face"—not a wavy line as you've done on other angry faces.

The eyes are large and the dots in the eyes are close together. Be careful not to draw the eyes as circles. They look more like the letter "D" lying on its side.

The nose looks like a fish hook.

This is a very different angry mouth. Instead of being open with the teeth showing, this mouth is closed. It's still easy to tell, however, that this character is angry!

Add a little wiggly line under his mouth to show his lower lip. Then draw the shoulders up high. On this character, the shoulders come up even a little HIGHER than the ears.

This little guy's mouth and eyebrows are going to be a little different. Begin by drawing a U-shaped head. Make the U-shape really wide. Add ears.

Draw a skinny neck that's curved a little. Add a collar to the end of the neck.

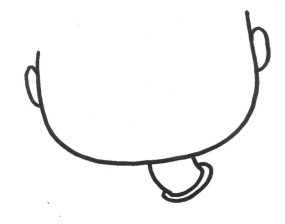

Next, draw some eyebrows. Notice that the eyebrows on this character are not wavy. Instead, they come to a point where they touch the top of the nose. It's almost like drawing the letter "V."

Draw the nose and the two eyes all about the same size.

Add shoulders.

The hair on this character is going to be short and spikey. Draw the hair the same way you would draw grass on the ground.

You can experiment a little with the length of the hair. Try it a little longer, then try it a little shorter.

Add some dots near the hairline to give the impression of hair that is very short or shaved.

The mouth turns down and no teeth are showing. Draw two lines that go from the side of the nose to the ends of the mouth. These are lines that some people get on their faces when they frown.

Below the mouth, add a wiggly line. This is the lower lip.

Add some dots on the sweater to give it texture.

Here are some other expressions that you can draw. Notice how some of the characters have their heads turned slightly to one side or the other.

Sick

Sad

Confused

Wacky

Evil

Proud

Impatient

Hairstyles—Male and Female

Try experimenting with different hairstyles on your characters. Here are some you might want to try...

Clothes, Costumes, and Uniforms

Sometimes you can tell what people do by what they are wearing. Here are some examples...

Partial Views

You don't always have to draw the whole character from head to toe. Sometimes you can just draw part of the character. Here are some examples of cartoons showing only partial views.

Peeking from behind a wall.

Sleeping in bed.

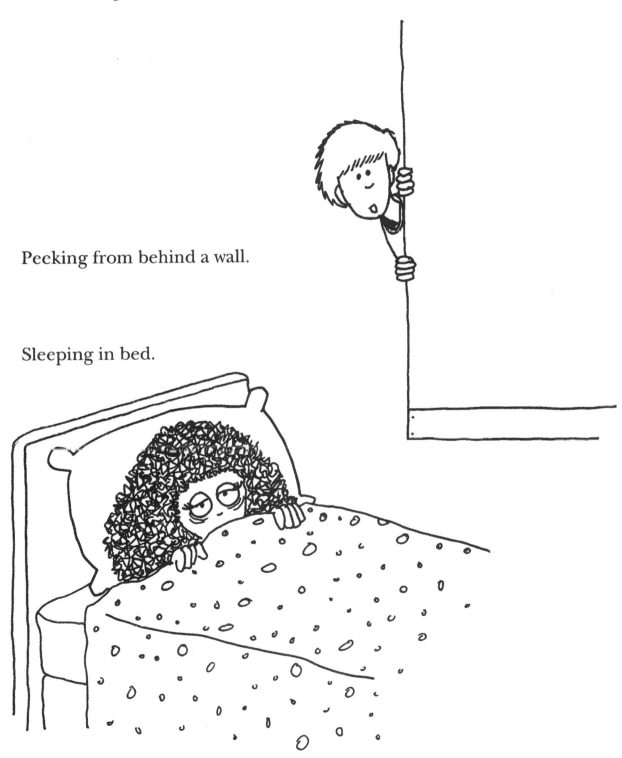

In a swimming pool or lake.

In a space station.

Body Shapes—Male

Here's one way to draw a simple male body. You can add your own face, hair, etc.

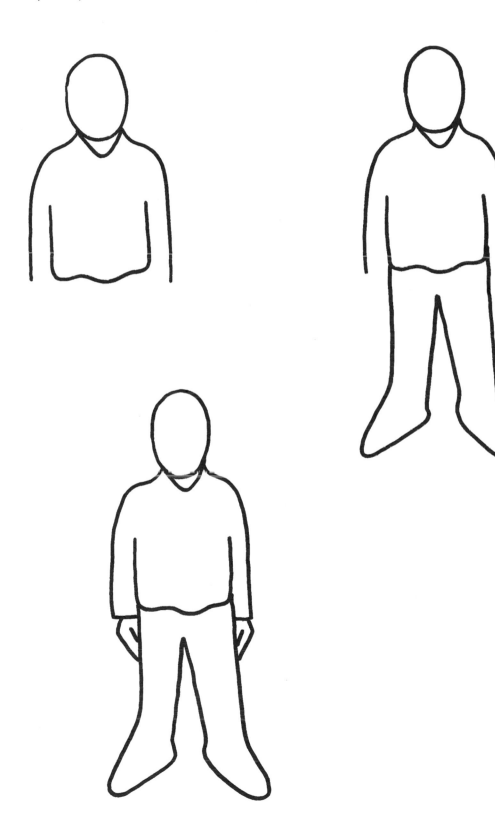

This cartoon character could probably lose a little weight…

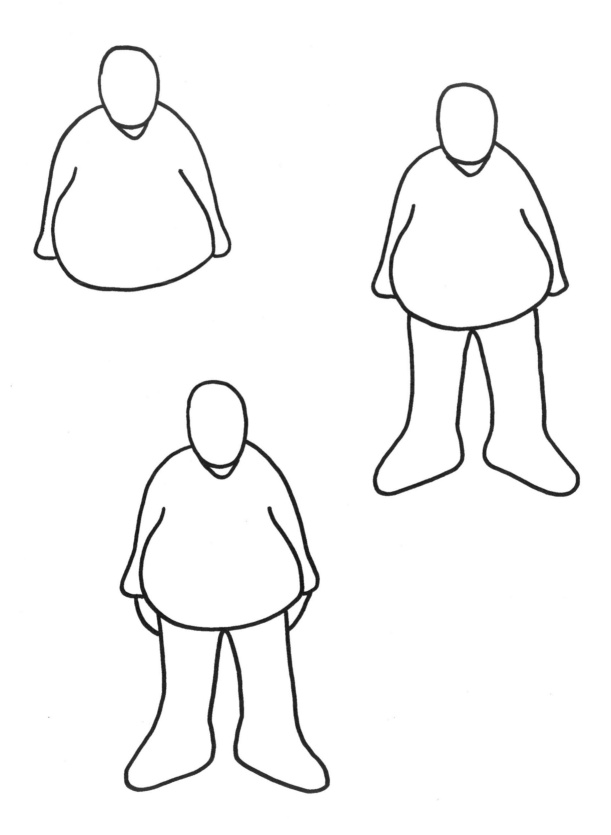

Body Shapes—Female

Here's a simple female body.

And here's how to draw an overweight female...

Body Shapes—Stretched

You can have some fun drawing people if you stretch the bodies as you draw them.

This tall character is drawn much like the previous average male character, but we've stretched the arms, trunk, and legs.

Often, beginning cartoonists draw arms too short. Keep in mind that the arms of your characters are almost always longer than you might think. Make them come down as far as the middle of the thigh.

Here's an example of a s-t-r-e-t-c-h-e-d female body.

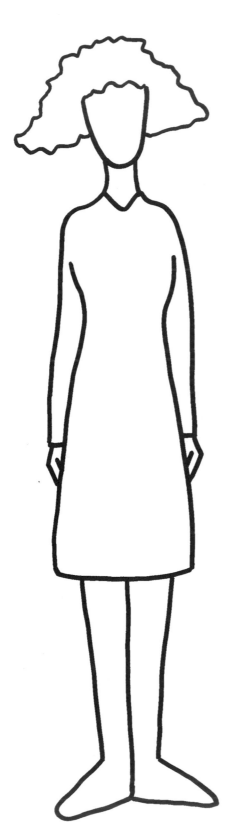

Once again, the trunk, arms, and legs have been extended to make her look very tall.

Body Shapes—Babies

Now we're going to go from tall, thin bodies to short, chubby bodies.

Babies are fun to draw. This little baby starts out as a smiley face with ears, arms, and hands. There's also a little curly hair on the baby's head.

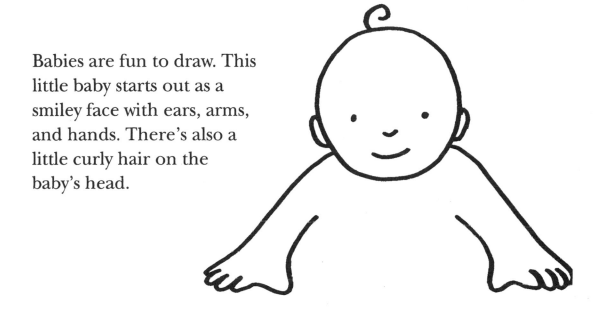

Notice how the arms come directly out of the baby's head. You don't need to draw the neck.

Next add a line around the baby's waist. Draw it from one arm across to the other arm. Then draw two peanut-shaped feet.

Add a big toe and four tiny toes on each foot.

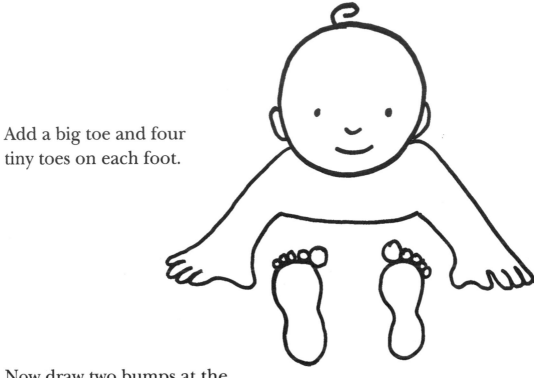

Now draw two bumps at the baby's waist to show the ends of the diaper.

Draw a curved line from each of the baby's thumbs to its feet. Then draw a curved line between the baby's feet. This is the bottom of the diaper.

Uh-oh, it looks like this baby has had a little accident!

Hands

Beginning cartoonists often have problems drawing hands. In this section, you'll learn how to draw several different kinds of hands. Some will look realistic, some will look very cartoony.

Begin by drawing a square.

Add a thumb on one side.

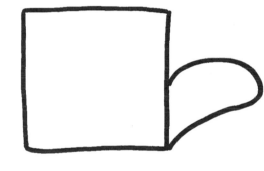

Now, add four "french fry" shapes onto the square palm.

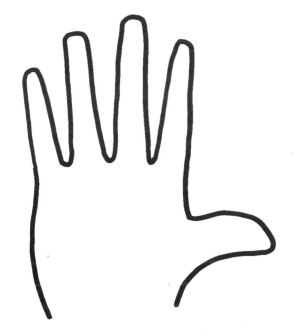

Erase the square shape that you started with. Round the ends of the fingers.

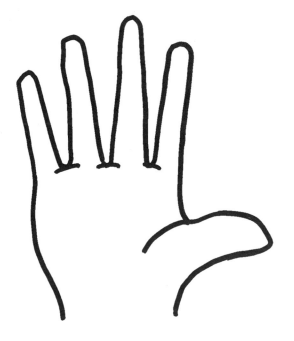

Add some little curved lines at the base of the fingers.

Now, extend the curved line of the thumb into the hand.

Presto! You've drawn a hand.

This is the right hand. If you want to draw the left hand, just put the thumb on the other side.

As you can see, this hand looks fairly realistic. Let's look at some other ways of drawing hands that are more cartoony.

This cartoon character has her hands at her sides.

By following steps 1, 2, and 3,
you can draw these simple
hands on your
cartoon characters.

Give it a try!

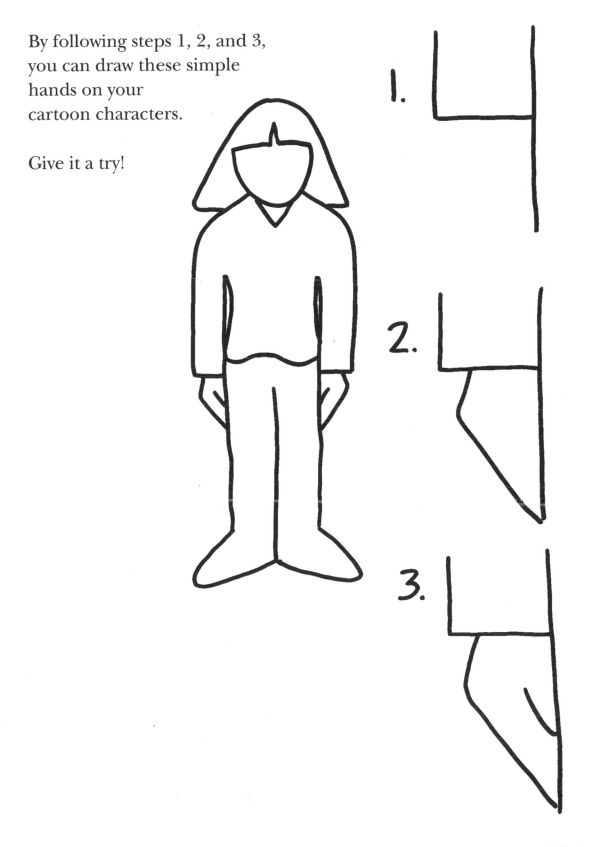

1.

2.

3.

This character has one hand on his hip and the other hand gesturing to the side.

Here's how to draw these kinds of hands…

1.

2.

3.

Hands Intertwined

Here's a way to draw hands intertwined.

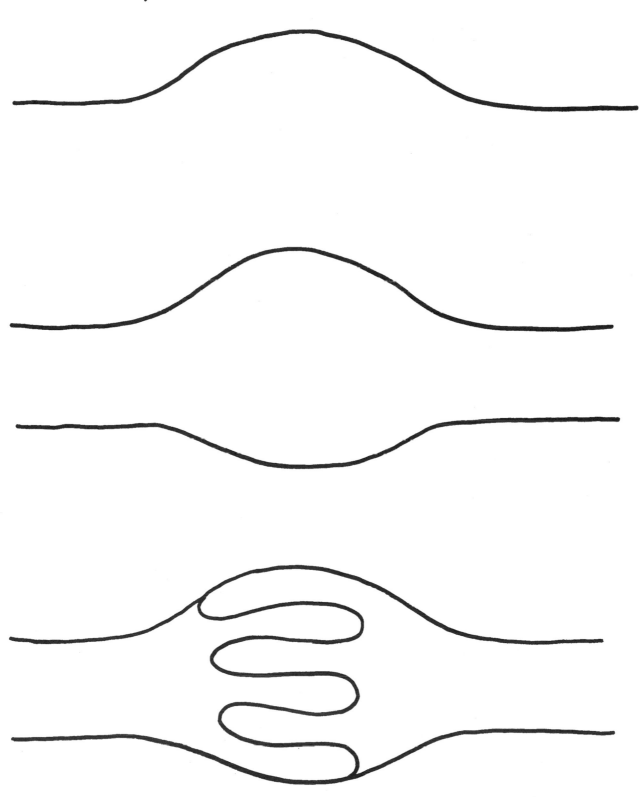

You can use intertwined hands in a number of ways. Here are two of them:

Opera star singing.

Businessperson at a desk.

Arms

You can create a lot of different "looks" by moving your characters' arms.

This girl has the simple extended hands we saw earlier. By drawing her arms in different positions, you can make her appear to be waving, gesturing, or waiting to give you a hug.

Try it for yourself. Draw the extended hands, then move the arms around, and see what kind of look you can give your cartoon characters.

Arms and Legs

These cartoon characters both have skinny arms and legs. Try experimenting with different thicknesses of arms and legs in your cartoons.

People Sitting

Sometimes you'll want to draw people sitting in chairs, on a sofa, or on the floor. Here are three cartoons showing people sitting.

If you can find photographs of people in those positions, it will help you see what happens to the human body when we sit.

Movement

So far, we've been drawing people standing or sitting still. Now we'll draw people in motion.

Since we're moving beyond simple shapes, the following cartoons will not have any step-by-step instructions. Instead, just draw what you see next to the numbered steps.

Step 1.

Step 2.

Step 3.

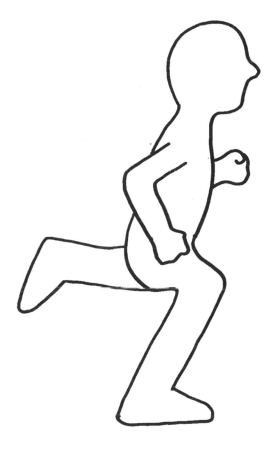

Step 4.

Motion Lines

Here are some cartoon characters involved in various sports.
Notice how motion is shown by using curved lines.

Here are some more sports characters. Notice how both have their tongues sticking out? That's one way to show "effort."

Unusual Positions

Both of these characters are in unusual positions while they are in motion.

When you want to draw cartoons like these, it helps to look at photographs of people in magazines or newspapers. It's not cheating to look at pictures to get ideas. Lots of artists use models to help them see how the human body looks in different positions.

You might even get a friend to pose for you so you can draw cartoons of people in unusual positions.

Caption Balloons
(sometimes known as "Speech Bubbles")

About the Author

Mike Artell has written dozens of books for children, their parents, and their teachers. Each year, he visits approximately 50 schools across the country, where he shares his techniques for thinking funny, writing funny, and drawing funny.

Mike also addresses educational conferences and conducts professional development workshops on the importance of using humor to enhance creativity.

For additional information, visit Mike's website: www.mikeartell.com

Index

Alligator, 6–8
Angry faces
    female, 75–82
    male, 91–98
Animals, 5–65
Arms and legs, 117–118
Babies, 109–110
Baby chicks, 25
Balloons, caption, 125–126
Baseball player, 122
Bear, 9–11
Beaver, 12–13
Bird, 14–15
Bison, 16–18
Boar, 52
Body shapes, 103–110
Buffalo, 16–18
Bunny, 19–20
Businessperson, 116
Caption balloons, 125–126
Carnivores, 60
Cat, 21–22
Chicken, 23–24
Chicks, 25
Clam, 26
Clothes, 100
Costumes, 100
Crab, 27–28
Diver, 122
Dog, 29–31
Dolphin, 32-33
Duck, 34–35
Effort, 123
Emotions, 82, 90, 98
Faces, smiling,
    female, 67–74
    male, 83–89
Female
    angry faces, 75–82
    body shapes, 105–106, 108
    smiling faces, 67–74
Fish, 36–37

Golfer, 123
Hairstyles, 99
Hands, 111–116
Hippopotamus, 38
Lagomorphs, 19
Legs, 118
Lion, 40
Male
    angry faces, 91–98
    body shapes, 103–104, 107
    smiling faces, 83–89
Monkey, 42
Motion lines, 122–123
Mouse, 44
Movement, 120–123
Opera star, 116
Owl, 46
Oyster, 26
Parrot, 48
Partial views, 101–102
Penguin, 50
Pig, 52
Porcupine, 54
Positions, unusual, 124
Primates, 42
River horse, 38
Sheep, 55–56
Sitting, 119
Skunk, 57
Smiling faces
    female, 67–74
    male, 83–89
Sow, 52
Sports, 122
Teeth, 79, 81, 85, 87, 88–89, 90, 93
Tennis player, 123
Tiger, 60
Tongue sticking out, 123
Turtle, 62
Uniforms, 100
Walrus, 64